the garden that you're growing

rachel h

The Garden That You're Growing.

Copyright © 2024 Rachel H

All rights reserved.

Other than brief excerpts for reviews and commentaries, no part of this book may be reproduced by any means without permission of the publisher.

ISBN: 978-0-6453272-3-6

eBook ISBN: 978-0-6453272-4-3

Cover Designer: Matthew Huckel
Floral illustrations by Grace Noboa
Orange illustration by Tati Bordiu

Editor: Eleana Norton
eleana.poetry@gmail.com

This book is published independently under the imprint ALittlePoetic Publishing.

For enquiries, visit rachelhuckel.com or email rachelhuckel@gmail.com

the garden
that you're
growing

contents

the dust you came from   9

the street that blooms   91

postscript   175

the story starts as a broken thing—
think less metamorphosis
and more clipped wing.

but still it takes flight,
weaving jagged lines across the sky—

it can't keep itself from falling,
but oh, look at it try.

the dust you came from

better days

it's been raining for weeks.
my neighbour is trying
to hang her damp fitted sheet
over the tiny clotheshorse
on her balcony.

trying to fit something too big
over bones that were not designed
to carry this weight.

she looks on the verge of tears.

it's okay, i want to say to her.

i've been praying for better days too.

empty pots

one august, i dreamt of growing a garden. every morning i looked out onto my balcony. its bare tiles. barren surfaces. if i blinked, i could picture pots taking over the space. a long, wooden table with strawberries covering the surface. ivy above. hydrangeas below.

but i pushed the dream aside. it asked something of me i did not have: time. tenderness.

the next august, i gave in to the dream. bought a collection of terracotta pots. i planted strawberries. ivy. hydrangeas. every morning i went out onto my balcony and watered the garden. but the soil was already sodden. it's one thing to dampen a dream. it's another to drown it.

i dumped out my plants. spent months crying tears over empty pots because trying only led to giving too much: time. tenderness.

yet, the next august,
i dreamt of a garden again.

again
again
again
again
again

again

how are you, really?

what can i say
except that i have
a paper boat heart
and lately i've been
swallowing oceans?

spaghetti

the spaghetti simmers on the stovetop.
we need to eat.
and time doesn't stop for
family members in hospital
or lost jobs
or a head full of heaviness,
does it?

time doesn't know
how to turn down the temperature.
how quickly cold water can
turn into a boiling pot.

and i know
everything will settle
eventually.

but for the moment,
i don't even care
that it is all
spilling
over
the
surface.

new message:

last night i had a nightmare that
you were dead. i wanted to call you
but rolled over instead.

can i be honest?

it's been hard for me to sleep.
there's just too much on my mind
to lie awake counting sheep. i miss
when we'd do that, i miss being
young and knowing that by morning
all my bad dreams would be gone.

can you keep a secret?

i'm just a little sad. but i don't want
you to worry, life's not going too
bad. remember when i thought
there were monsters under my bed?
well, i've been thinking a lot about
what you said.

you were right about the monsters:
they're all in my head.

architecture

i am a house no longer holding up,
not what they call good bones.
there is rubble all around me
from walls once made of stone.

call it a force of nature
but the hurricane's from within.
i am folding under the weight
of a roof that was paper thin.

everything i'm composed of
is either too heavy or too light.
i'm the architect of my own chaos
because i can't get the balance right.

well, it's all coming down now,
the walls are deconstructing,
tapping forcefully on my shoulder
but i'm relieved they're interrupting.

i was stuck in a picture-perfect house
that i worked so hard to build.
and now that it's falling apart
i could not be more thrilled.

want to help me self-destruct?
take me apart brick by brick.
i am throwing each belief at the wall
and i can't make anything stick.

my walls have turned to weapons
that i am wielding in my hands,
too reckless with a pain
that i just can't understand.

i think i may be hurting people
but crumbling too fast to check,
shocked by the kind of honesty
that can be salvaged from this wreck.

i am trying to hold my ground
but not one punch is landing.
i don't know how to end a fight
and be the last one standing.

i wish i were a better person
with much more to offer you.
but i can't reverse time or rebuild
so i don't know what else to do.

by now i've gotten real good
at tucking all the mess away,
even fooled myself into thinking
that everything was okay.

i'm exhausted from pretending
this house can go back together—
when it's a knock down job today
but tomorrow it'll look "all better".

continents

i carried my suitcase across continents.
bruises began to blossom on
my calves, my thighs.
i said i didn't know where they came from,
but really,
i just didn't want to admit
i was too weak to carry the weight.

there was a lot to unpack.
but i kept my luggage locked.
i said i was keeping people out,
but really,
i just didn't want to let myself in.

i turned my head out the window.
traded blue skin for skies.
i said i was enjoying the view,
but really,
i just didn't want to press on anything
that could cause pain.

i carried my heart across continents.
how long can you hold a heavy thing
before you have to be honest about
how much it hurts?

irony

i'm touching up my self-portrait
to paint a better version of me,
when insufferably self-absorbed
is the one thing i'm trying not to be.

rose-coloured

your words in my ear so sickly sweet
that i feel stuck inside your honey.
if you have only nice things to say,
i'm afraid you don't really love me.

you're so numbed by infatuation
i'm not the girl you would have sworn.
you wrap your hands around my roses
and never once acknowledge the thorns.

your fingers bind my stems like twine,
but i cannot keep standing upright.
please take me down from that trellis.
let me out of that rose-coloured light.

i did not prune the branches when i should have.

i am my own consequence.

bad fruit

it's harvest season.

my labour has finally produced something beautiful. i can't deny that. the fruit is good. the fruit is sweet. i want to share it with others.

what i'm struggling to understand is why i am also harvesting things that leave a bitter taste in my mouth. why there is so much bad fruit.

i nurtured things that are now swollen and sour and i don't really know what to do with them. it's too painful to cut them out now. their roots are too deep.

bad fruit falls and something even worse grows in its place. all i think is *i am not good. i am not good. i am not good.* and i don't want you to know me. because i can't hand you the good fruit without the bad tumbling along with it.

my life is abundant. i stretch my arms in the morning and so much shakes out. but i gather all of it. *keep it to myself. keep to myself. keep myself.* because beauty is here. but so is shame. and i just can't seem to surrender it.

sunday stories

i've spent a lot of time trying to be good.
a good _____.
a good _____.
the nouns don't really matter.

yet in my practice of self-assessment
i am uncovering parts of my heart
that are ugly.

i have _____.
i have _____.
the verbs don't really matter.

someone asked me to pray and i asked if
someone else could do it because
i wasn't feeling well.

but the sickness was shame.
the first thing it does is separate.

one of the first-ever stories tells of
humans trying to hide themselves from God.
we are still writing our own renditions.

i don't think i can take out the ugly
without filling in the spaces with good.
i don't think i can find good
anywhere but at the feet of God.

so i sat with him for an hour.
told him all the things i'd uncovered.
all the parts of me that are unworthy,
unlovable.

he listened and listened
and when he was sure i had finished telling him
all about who i was,
he asked if i'd like to hear a little about who he is.

he told me the greatest story of all time.
another one that is not new.
i've heard it before.
i've heard it over and over.

                                              God, can you tell it to me again?

the greatest story of all time

then you said, "let there be light."
it was good. then it wasn't.
but, one day, it will be again.

you created the shape of the sea,
placed creatures teeming within it.
you form things before you fill them.

we rocked the boat and waves arose.
it was good. then it wasn't.
but, one day, it will be again.

Jesus, you came to meet us
right in the middle of it.
you walk on waves before you still them.

then you said, "my burden is light."
i was good. then i wasn't.
but, because of you, i am again.

you created the shape of your story,
placed us to live within it.
you form promises before you fulfil them.

this is the greatest story of all time.
it was good. then it wasn't.
but, one day, it will be again.

truth

Jesus was there at my
lowest point of self-esteem,
but he was also there at my
highest.

it was then that he called me to examine
the worst parts of me.

not to tear me down
(though it may have looked like that at first).
rather to build me back up
with a sense of confidence that is founded
in truth.

who i am in Jesus
will always be firmer than
the fickle forms of confidence
that i had used to console myself,
covering up my walls with
thick coats of paint
any time the
story
started
chipping.

built to break

i used to think my heart
was a broken wind-up toy—
a manufacturing error
that God forgot to destroy.

why else would it be that,
even when it's not wound,
it can't help but glitch with
its obnoxious built-in sound.

i carry it in my chest,
a little nervous every day
that it'll embarrass me by picking
the wrong moments to play.

it just keeps going off
at the worst possible times—
when i'm on my way to work
or in supermarket lines.

i used to ask God
to fix the faulty thing he made,
to replace it with a heart
that is far better behaved.

but lately i've been thinking
that i've gotten it all wrong—
what if God uses the brokenness
so people can hear the song?

what if my heart only broke
in all the places it's been
because it was calling me to people
i never would have seen?

what if the sound doesn't mean
i wasn't put together right,
and the cracks in my composition
only let in more light?

what if i loved my little heart,
even if it was built to break,
and lived each day unashamed
of the music that it makes?

music

i am my own harshest critic.

i can't take shelter from the thunderstorm
long enough for the water to evaporate.
        for the words to lose their weight.

i spend my nights drowning in the day:
how it feels to be forgotten. or worse,
        how it feels to be remembered.
the gaps i shouldn't have filled. or worse,
        the spaces i should have.

but grace is a shapeshifter.

lately, it's been meeting me
as the tin roof between
me and the sky.

so even when

> the
> words
> are
> bucketing
> down

    i am safe and dry.

i don't hear every reason
i am not good enough.

i just hear a lullaby.

light of grace

your design is not flawed.
you don't need to go against the grain of
your own make-up.

you only need to surrender yourself
to be transformed under
the bright and holy shine of Jesus' face.

your weaknesses are your greatest strengths
when held up to the light of grace.

a letter from my thirteen-year-old self

I planted a garden.
A garden of negative thinking, fear and stress.
So I grew crops of impossible thinking
I will never be good enough.
I am afraid/worried
Life is too hard.
And I watered them day after day.
But then the farmer came.
He pulled out the weeds and planted
seeds of hope, love and faith
So crops grew of joy, peace and goodness.
I can do anything through Christ.
I am joyful / thankful.
It is well with my soul.
Everyday he comes to water my garden.
He prunes it to grow more fruit.
In the winter he protects it
In the summer it never dries up.
O watch over my garden, Father + Lord.

the garden that you're growing

you're looking in the mirror
and don't like what you see.
you're nothing like the person
that by now you thought you'd be.

and the voices in your head
start telling you those lies,
now there's a tremor in your lip
and tears inside your eyes.

they tell you about the others
who are so much better than you,
and you've heard it enough times
that you start to believe it's true.

that everything you've worked to be
and everything you've made
when put against another life
just all begin to fade.

but oh, you need to wipe your eyes
to see things as they are.
a life of your own making
should never be put on par.

and their grass just may be greener
but that is not worth knowing.
for the greenest grass cannot compare
to the garden that you're growing.

i am convinced we are made up
of the stories we tell ourselves.

rewrite.

measure miracles

we try to measure miracles
like rainfall on dry land.
you can read the numbers on the gauge,
but oh, see how the flowers stand.

and if you are that miracle
(and i'm telling you, you are),
you might think you don't measure up,
but oh, see how you've come so far.

wild imagination

there is a tree in my grandparents' yard. when i was little i used to believe that fairies lived there. i used to climb it to try and find them. i don't believe in fairies anymore. but i still climb the tree because i know that the little girl with her wild imagination is still there. and i believe in her.

what would you say to your younger self?

it's a leading question. i know it should be of some reassurance. something about how you'll get through the confusion, the pain, the wrong. you won't. it'll still baffle you in twenty years' time how people can do bad things. only, you'll do a few of your own, and girl, wait till you try to wrap your head around that.

i know i should say you'll outgrow those blue butterfly pyjamas. that you'll get to leave things behind. you won't. you will still cocoon yourself in sheets when you're trying to work things out. still fly far away in your mind when you don't like where your body is. i know it should be a promise. or, at the very least, an apology. but it's not. this is all i would say: *i want to be just like you when i grow up.*

honest

i am longing for the kind of honesty i can embody.
i yearn to have honest hands that do honest things.
which can hand over weight to share when it is all too
much for me to hold. i want to have honest eyes.
which see things how they really are, not just how i
want to see them. and if that means i cry, may those
tears be as honest as they can be. please let me have
an honest mouth. that can say, "i think i've gotten it
wrong this time." "i am still learning how to love."
"can we at least try to mend this before we leave?"

i am desperate to be honest. even when—especially
when—the world has not been honest with me.

entry-level human

i don't exactly know what it is i have to offer here. i'm not entirely confident in my talents—despite what my polished resume will tell you.

so for now i am making my occupation an entry-level human. i am learning on the job. i am in the business of being kind. but i make mistakes often, still. i am using the degree i have in invisibility to be a listening ear. a well-placed word. sometimes i work from the comfort of my own home and other times i travel, but regardless, the dress code is always to wear my heart on my sleeve.

and you can call me whatever job title you want to, but the one thing i hope you can never call me is dishonest.

whose way are we doing this?

there is a grey couch in our living room
where i go to meet God each morning.

i bundle myself up with a tea
and a ridiculously large
orange blanket and
read his word.

i've done this for a while now—
nearly every day since we got
the couch.

and each morning, i bring
the same fear before God.

it comes in different forms:
sometimes a prayer.
sometimes a poem.
sometimes a stubborn silence.

but over and over again,
i am pleading with God
for purpose.

for a line of work that acknowledges
my passions, for people whom i can help,
for direction in my creativity.

it's a little ironic
because i want to serve God (i do),
but when i come to him like this,

i am really asking him
to serve me.

devotion

reading your bible is a sign of devotion
but so is sitting with a friend in
the still of the night,
putting pen to paper every morning
no matter how uninspired you are,
filling the sugar pot in the kitchen
when it's running low,
walking the same route with
the same dog at dusk,
being faithful with everything
God has placed in your care.

this is a way of worship too.

the work

i asked God for productivity
and he gave me
meandering walks around the neighbourhood,
poems on my heart every morning,
tender thoughts to pick apart like dandelions and
watch how they scatter on the breeze.

i asked God how i can serve
and he gave me
spontaneous messages from friends asking to meet,
unexpected conversations with even more
unexpected people,
odd ideas for shared adventures that came over me
like a fever.

i asked God to glorify himself
and he gave me
a garden on my balcony to grow,
dirt under my fingernails as i daily examined
the soil from which things may bloom.

i keep giving myself to God;
God gives me joy and beauty
and tells me

this is the work too.

back to life

occasionally,
when i am not clawing at life,
not turning over every stone
trying to find my purpose,
i remember to live it.

little sunflower,

how your heart longs to grow tall.
and you spend your days reaching
towards the broke-open sky,
pushing yourself to prove that
you can make something
out of yourself, rise above
the dust you came from.
you pray faithfully for purpose
but never posture.
that is your folly, little flower.
to think that you need to do
anything but awake
to greet the fresh mercies of
the morning, and expectantly
turn your face towards
the Son.

big red shoes

to the girl cloaked in red,
my, those are some big shoes.
you stepped into another role—
what do you have to prove?

you've been huffing like a wolf
to keep up with your own ambition.
but is this really what you wanted?
to whose voice did you listen?

to the girl with red ribbons,
watch out for those big bad lies.
they'll come back to bite you
but they'll be dressed as wise.

they told you you could do things
so you thought it meant you should.
and you ran far in the wrong shoes
just to show yourself you could.

to the girl in the mirror, mirror,
it's easy to get your tales twisted.
tell me, was it courage or pride:
the real reason you persisted?

uncloak your weighty ambition.
shake out your tightly wound hair.
untie your big red shoes—
try a more fitting pair.

unseen

in a dream, i stumbled upon a garden growing by the water. i was on the run from something, but the beauty of the garden slowed me down. my running shoes sunk into the soft soil, and i strolled through, stopping to touch the fruit hanging overhead.

i thought, 'who has tended to this eden? who would care so much for creation that they are committed to growing something on public land? do they not want to be known? do they not want to taste the fruits of their labour instead of giving it over to people who will never know how it came to be? don't they want to know that i found the garden, and it became a refuge for my tired feet?'

i considered how in my waking life i had nurtured visions in which i was so prominently seen. from that day i asked God: restore in me a new dream.

less

what if one day i woke up and asked God to make me less?

the envelope

an older woman
paying for her many books
digs through her purse
and pulls the world out.

in there is an envelope
marked 'TSAB'.

i know i shouldn't
ask her about it.
but my curiosity
gets the better of me.

she tells me it stands for
twin separated at birth.
that it was sent to her
by a friend she feels
is a kindred spirit.

in the envelope
is a birthday card
and a one-hundred-dollar note.

for decades they have been
sending one another money

but not to keep.

the money is to carry
on their person.
for God to give them
the opportunity
to bless someone
who crosses their path.

i know i shouldn't
read into it.
but my overthinking
gets the better of me.

what would it look like
to equip someone to become
the blessing that,
with God,
they can be?

minding my business

people i love.
words i've said.
work i've done.
things i own.
eventually, i have to let it all go.

they have their own journeys
independent of me
like this poem that will be read
in rooms i will never see.

nothing in this life
is ever truly mine—
God just gives them to me
to mind for a time.

i try to mind my business
when it's time for them to move on.
i don't need to know where they land
to know care given is never gone.

just enough

will i trust you to clear the path just enough for me to take my next step? or will i try to hack down everything in sight for miles?

the war on waiting

i admit, i am no good
at waiting.

i try to kick down
closed doors and
yank the leaves from
trees in autumn.

i throw myself at
daydreams and wake up
dizzy from the
blunt force of desire.

some days i wonder,
what if i wasn't so
brutal?

what if i stopped
bruising my heart
by battling
for what it wants?

is it possible to keep
the dreams i've been given
and simply wait,
instead of going to war?

own pace

take a deep breath, it's okay
to have dreams you do not chase.
some hopes are planted seeds
needing to grow at their own pace.

garden bed

on an early winter morning,
i rose from my bed
and tip-toed outside,
quietly sliding the screen door
closed behind me.

i tucked my feet into gumboots
and crept over to check
on my beloved garden.

the soil was sleeping.

nothing growing,
no toil beneath the surface.

it's been a long year.
one of profound productivity,
constant creation.

i thought it only took a toll
on me.

but when the gardener rests,
the soil sighs in relief

and sleeps happily
in the garden bed.

nurture

when the harvest is abundant,
i am tempted to go shallow.
i don't need to put in deep work
when the stores have not yet run low.

now i am learning the hard way
to love when the land is fallow.
plough nourishment into the ground,
nurture with time before i sow.

figuring out
how to use an abundance
is worship.

figuring out
how to use an absence
is faith.

which is your devotion born from?

patient in the old

sometimes you have to go out into unknown places
to find the story you want to be part of. other times,
you have to stay in the familiar to write it yourself.
you need to be patient in the old in order to give
birth to something new.

flighty

what is it about humans
that make us such
restless creatures?

we want to go out,
then swiftly want to go home.

we want company,
only to crave being alone.

we want the freedom of no ties,
to be like birds in the wind.
only to realise that
they too need a place to
rest their wings.

still your flighty heart.

why are you so eager
to be anywhere
but here?

discontent

in the night i wake up restless.
i roll out of one dream and into another,
always finding some reason to forsake
a certain fantasy and fall asleep again
to start from scratch.

i live my days the same.

and if i am feeling restless,
it's because i need God to
ground me.

or because i have walked
into a place of fear and
complacency and he is
shaking me, saying,

move.

you are not a disaster

you are not a disaster for your desire.
you are allowed to want things with
a force that takes you by surprise.
it is okay to be discontent
with your environment.
to dig up soil and pull up plants
and start the whole thing over.

you are not reckless for your wanting.
it is okay to make big changes
and take risks and
wipe out flowers with the weeds.

you are not a disaster,
but even if you were,
sometimes havoc is what the heart needs.

the prayer plant on my desk
has outgrown its pot.

if i repot it, it might die.
but if i don't, it will rot.

each night i watch the leaves close,
pointed upwards in prayer.

i hold the same faith
that i can flourish

elsewhere.

spring

not much happens in your comfort zone.

you must throw off
the blanket of snow
you've been sleeping under
if you ever want a
shot at spring.

how much time do you have?

> "my son's name is jonah."
> "that's a beautiful name."
> "doesn't your bible have a story about
> someone with the name jonah?"
> "it does. it's a bit of a crazy story."
> "something to do with a whale?"
> "how much time do you have?"

the older i get, the more i understand
the story. how easy it is to run away.

i understand the attempt to outrun
a God who holds the earth in his palms.

i understand the reasoning that maybe
a God who's never once failed to
fulfil a promise will forget about
the thing he's asked of me.

it's worth a shot.

i can't say i've spent three days
in the stomach of a great fish.

but i can say i've spent years
trying to quieten the thunderous call
that kept me from my sleep.

this is how i'd summarise jonah's story
(and how i'd summarise mine):

obedience isn't always easy.

but it is inevitable.

                                          God's got the time.

palms

my palms are learning a thing or two
about worship.
sweaty and shaking, they are
made beautiful.
learning that you do not
have to wait for strength to serve
when the one you are serving is
infinitely stronger.

strong enough

if a butterfly doesn't struggle to come out of its cocoon, it'll never be strong enough to fly.

imagine

i don't thirst for small dreams anymore;
i seek only visions.

when i think of change, it's not
a flower growing in the desert;
there are forests on those plains.

the very moment i came to Jesus
he made my barren heart
beautiful.

imagine what he will do with a lifetime.

laughter

sometimes i wonder if God created the kookaburra just so he can laugh at us. we never have any idea what he is about to do. he's spoken things into existence since the beginning of time. but listen— he's still doing something new.

loose threads

we have a God who works behind the scenes,
weaving so many stories together
that you'd never think of how they
could possibly intertwine—

until they do.

my favourite storytellers

God loves to write stories that take a long time to unfold. days. decades. the entire life span of humankind.

think of sarah—how she waited ninety years to have a child. a child whose family line would welcome the Saviour of the world.

and yet Jesus had a short life. his ministry unfolding in just three years. think of the five thousand—how Jesus broke bread to feed them. responding to the needs he saw in the moment.

if God is a slow storyteller,
Jesus is a spontaneous one.

what else can i say to your wrestling heart?

be patient. be ready.

unstructured

you want to know you're serving God
so you make yourself a plan.
you block out time every week
and then wash it off your hands.

you go to your allotted ministry
at the church building each week.
because you want to check a box
instead of letting God speak.

and maybe God does want you
to serve him in the way you do,
but maybe if you slowed you'd see
he has other tasks for you.

maybe there's a person
you'll cross paths with today
that you could help if you weren't so busy
looking the other way.

maybe there's an opportunity
that will fit just your skills,
but you're so distracted you let it pass
and the position never fills.

this is not to say
that the way you're doing things is wrong,
and God cannot be silenced
by the schedules you follow along.

but at some point you must admit
that busyness is a choice,
and ask yourself, in the status quo,
are you listening to his voice?

surrender

i want to be open to God today.
and what he may want to say.
and how he may want to move.
i don't want such a firm grip on my life
that i can't allow myself to be surprised.

because if i really thought
God were the better storyteller,
i wouldn't tell him about my plans
and ask him to bless them.

i would ask him to wreck them.

for beth

beth,
you are the hardest worker
i know.

if it were up to me,
i'd give you a raise.
but you don't work for me.
instead you're just
one of my best friends,
which means a good title
but no pay and
too much responsibility.

you say you can only be around
people who can keep up with you,
but let me tell you, that's no easy feat.

you walk as though you're running late
and you speak as though your mouth is
tripping on the pace at which your
mind is running.

what do you get when
two overachievers travel together?
no one sleeps in,
we spend that time
with our heads tucked in spreadsheets.

i tried to keep up,
but by six am you'd created
three options for the day
and made it clear we weren't doing
plan b or c.

beth,
you are so competent
it makes me redundant.
let me explain what i mean.

each morning i left the hotel
without a care.
you had our tickets.
you had our maps.
you had our room key.

and i learned to relax
day by day
as i trusted you to get us
where we needed to be.

beth,
you asked me
what it means to have faith
and what it is about God i believe.

well, i can teach you,
but beth,
you're also teaching me.

i've trusted God for many years,
and he's proved his faithfulness,
but it's only recently
that i've learned the fullness
of what it is for him to lead.

he holds all my days in his hands,
has a well-thought-out plan.
what is left for me to do
but not worry?

beth,
when you trust God,
life changes
unexpectedly.

i have a foolish amount of fun
on any given day,
just as i had frolicking
around foreign cities.

beth,
you are the best analogy
of what life with God could be.

i once thought that following
meant i was locked down.
now i've learned
i'm free.

possibility

the day tumbles in
crisp and fresh
like laundry from the dryer and
i wonder about all the ways
in which to wear it.

zest

i don't sleep that much anymore.
i know it's something i should work on.
but how am i to say goodnight
when i am holding out for dawn?

i wake up at four am
impatient to start my day.
i once loved to stretch my sleep
but its length now gets in my way.

and maybe i'm just delirious
from not getting enough rest,
but my whole life is christmas eve—
a return of a nearly lost zest.

picture

i fell in love with stories
when i was five years old
and given a new book
that was my own to hold.

between the glossy pages
were images of dreamy lands:
unicorns and magic doors
all in my little hands.

i saw a mirror turn to water
as children slid right through,
their tiny worlds expanding
as they discovered one so new.

a land of jewels and flowers,
of blue and rainbow skies.
you could see the awe and wonder
illustrated in their eyes.

i am still in love with stories,
and if i'm honest, i still believe
that there are two sides to everything:
lifted hands on bent knees.

sometimes my mirror turns to water
as i slip in between
the world that is in front of me
and the one behind the scenes.

i am always illustrating
ideas of what could be:
something i can picture
but not something i can see.

just please be patient with me,
i hope there's beauty ahead,
as i spend my life building you
the worlds that are in my head.

unearth

there is something in me that wonders: have i actually changed? or has this always been who i am and i'm just finding it for the first time?

déjà rêvé

everything feels completely different
but also slightly the same.
there is a certain familiarity
that is very hard to name.
it's like a scent from your childhood
that you can't quite put your finger on.
there is something now returning
that i had thought was lost and gone.
things have certainly been changing,
and i now feel i have at last
suddenly arrived at the place
that i have dreamed of in the past.

present

once, God woke me up from a dream
just to tell me it was happening.

the days feel different

the days feel different lately.

there is a childlike spirit in me
that i have long since put to bed
in favour of things like
work and wisdom
(which carry their own kind of goodness).

but she is waking up from her slumber
and demanding things like
the right to play,
the right to make a mess,
and, most importantly,
the right to believe not only
that miracles may happen,

but that they will.

mess is just creativity
overgrown.

out of control

i traded my concrete ambitions
for wildflower dreams.
my garden is overgrowing,
but isn't it the most beautiful thing you've seen?

our summer is not for sale

we've spent enough time trying to be wise.
we're so "wise" now, it is making us foolish.

we nearly spent our day
hunched over spreadsheets, moving numbers
around so we can get ourselves
one of those mortgages, move apartments.

we've worked hard to get here.
(but did we have to?)
there's no rush to find the money.
(we'll be doing it for decades.)

and my love, i am just not ready
to sell another summer.
not yet.

so for now, it's a beautiful spring day.

let's head down to the ocean.
come back sun-kissed and salty and

love until the light goes down.
(love until our limbs give out.)

i want to spend the evening
resting my foolish bones
beside yours,
in our home—

beach towels hanging
over the balcony, clothes
crumpled on the floor.

we are happy here, my love.

what more could we possibly need?

coming of age

i outgrew the books
i read in my teens,
the plots no longer a place
my story could be seen.

i outgrew the angst,
outgrew the adventure,
traded them for discipline
towards more grown-up ventures.

i wrote emails in one breath,
made money while i slept,
so constantly active
that passivity crept.

not embarking on quests,
i perfected routines,
running in circles
instead of writing new scenes.

but that is all changing,
i am tearing up The Plan,
tracing my passions back
to where they began.

rediscovering spontaneity,
returning my attention
to the people i lost
in the fog of clear intention.

i am losing myself
in other people's stories,
letting myself adventure
in unchartered territories.

this chapter is for unlearning
all my so-called wise ways.
perhaps this is a rite of passage too:
this great un-coming of age.

the street that blooms

responsibility

my neighbourhood is a patchwork
of grasses unruly and well-kept.
for we can't agree if maintaining
the sidewalk strip is an overstep.

should i keep to myself
or risk crossing their lines?
if no one has responsibility,
how much of it is mine?

new town

i'm making a lot of friends;
i'm not making any memories.

i have a lot of memories
with friends i don't see anymore.

i don't want to go back
but it's hard to move forward.

my social life has stalled.

recount

if i go to one more coffee catch-up,
i think i'm going to scream.
i'm sick of hearing about lives
lived individually.

i don't want to talk about
another month i wasn't a part of.
i can tell you what i did in mine:
just repeats of the above.

and i know it's bad to say,
i know it seems like i don't care;
i do care about your life,
i just wish that i was there.

i get our lives are oh so full
with our Very Important Plans,
but how play became playing catch-up
i'll never understand.

if i get asked 'what's new?' once more,
i really think i might yell.
i'm just so busy telling stories
i have no stories to tell.

so hear me out on this one:
what if we hit ignore?
leave behind our responsibilities
and just go and explore?

we can take our coffee to go,
stroll aimlessly through the town,
and get all kinds of lost as we find
new avenues to wander down.

lie down with me in the grass,
look up with me to the sky.
our lives move on so fast,
we can't let the moment drift by.

let's make each other laugh
until our stomachs start to ache,
and make up our own tales
from the cloud's familiar shape.

it's rare to see you face to face
so let's do heart to heart,
and just enjoy the time together
not recount the time apart.

play

let's dangle our legs over
the end of a pier.
drive through the night and let
the conversation steer.

split a bottle of wine and walk
giddily through the streets.
chat by the ocean,
wet sand under our feet.

adult friendships are hard,
but do you think we make it that way?

what if i called and just asked you
to come over and play?

i don't want your perfect friendship.

i don't want neatly wrapped gifts on my birthday and well-spaced coffee dates and a dozen frameable photos.

i want your texts at three in the morning when you feel alone. i want to come with you to the grocery store when life gets too busy to catch up. i want you to tell me the truth about how many times you've gone to the bathroom just to catch a breath.

i don't want your consistency; i want to be inconvenienced. i want you to call me on a sunday night before bed when i haven't heard from you in weeks. i want to be there when you need me and be there when you're just dropping in to say hello.

i don't want your perfect friendship.
i want real friendship.
i want you.

dilemma

my little sister asks me
for help with her maths homework
and i find myself mad at my memory.

i can't believe that high school algebra
still takes up space when
there is not enough room to store
the names of my closest friends' siblings.

i can't believe i can solve textbook equations
but could never figure out
how to show people that i'm there.

i hand messages in like overdue maths homework
and hope they read,
'i'm sorry it's late. but i love you. i care.'

a confession

i let the car battery go flat.
pretended not to know what flowers
you can plant in full sun.
"forgot" the word i was looking for.
knew the dress i tried on would look
hideous on me.

when people are hurting, a lot of the time,
they will need something.

but sometimes,
they just need
to be needed.

the distance

a) the other day, my train got delayed and i remembered that one time it happened to you on your way to the airport. how you asked any strangers holding suitcases if they wanted to get an uber to the airport with you. i was about to ask the girl behind me the same thing. we were city bound, and she was running late for her exam. only, the train took off and for some reason i was disappointed. we might have been strangers, but we were both human. (the distance does not matter.)

b) i remember when you spoke about bravery not long before you moved. you quoted *we bought a zoo* and how sometimes you just need twenty seconds of insane courage. it made me laugh because you were only quoting it in the context of biting into a bruised apple. but the way we do the little things is how we learn to do the big ones. (the distance does not matter.)

c) i don't know what to send you in the mail. sometimes a heartfelt letter. sometimes a picture. or a +4 uno card. there is so much potential in a postage stamp. what do i send that says i am proud of the parts of myself that are becoming more like you? (the distance does not matter.)

figuring out
how to use an abundance
is play.

figuring out
how to use an absence
is resourcefulness.

which is your creativity born from?

art is our ambassador.

it stands in for us when we cannot find the words we want to say. it's why we share concert videos and playlists and quotes we've underlined in our books. we are saying, 'these lyrics are part of me' or 'these poems make up who i am'.

when art is exchanged, it becomes an ambassador for all the unspoken words between people. it's why neither of us need to say anything when my husband starts playing our wedding song on his guitar. or why a friendship can survive on just messages back and forth with pictures that 'made me think of you'.

and when art is adopted by the other person, it stands in the space between them. so that it feels like there's no space between them at all. name a more intimate love language than 'i learned to play your favourite song on the piano' or 'i read the book you mentioned last week'.

art is our ambassador. we can say nothing at all and still find a way to speak.

translate

if you listen carefully, people are always telling you the languages they want to be loved in.

birthday cake

you're reaching a milestone birthday
and don't know what to do.
you know you're meant to have a party
but it doesn't really feel like you.

you worry if you do something big
they'll think you're over the top.
but if you don't invite people
no one will remember to show up.

you may think your day's a lost thing
amid the chaos of december.
but i want to tell you why
it's a day i will always remember.

you showed me the joy
of lives lived side by side:
our celebrations multiply
and our burdens divide.

i don't think of my successes
as something done on my own.
and when i fail miserably
i know i am not alone.

your friendship is a gift
that blesses my life every day.
and on your upcoming birthday
i'd like to celebrate you in some way.

we could just dig our forks
into a grocery store cake.
or we could make one ourselves
if you have the patience to bake.

hands folded into flour
as the clock ticks to midnight
and i sing poorly to you
by birthday candle light.

i am bad at many things,
but i don't want one to be loving you.
so if you have anything in mind,
just say the word, that's what we'll do.

going into my twenties, i wanted to be on everyone's team. playing alongside them. never missing the moments when they scored. always open for them to pass to if needed—the perfect teammate.

i was not honest with myself about how much energy i had for people. i started missing games. kept dropping the ball. felt guilty for not being there. resentful when i was. guilty about being resentful.

i needed a time-out.

now there are fewer people i do life with. but that does not mean i have lost love for others. not at all. i am still on your team. it just looks a little different now. i don't go to your games but i still wear your colours. yes, not always *with* you. but, and i need you to know this,

always rooting *for* you.

different paths

you chose wings;
i chose roots.

i don't think we ever
forgave each other
for that. but we
are trying.

and look at us now.

with your wings, you
are growing;
with my roots, i
am flying.

central perk

i met this girl
who loved the show *friends*
so much that she
wanted to create her
own version of
central perk.

so she hand-selected
five other people
and invited them to
a dive bar each
wednesday night.

then she started to
meet them there
at other times
throughout the week,
individually
or together.

when an apartment
in her building
became available,
she talked to the landlord and
tried to convince her friends
to move in.

and i get it.

we all want people
we can meet at the end
of a long day.
we all want a place
to feel like home.

but if we stop searching
for friendship that feels
effortless, we may just find
that the effort is the thing
holding us together.

not all friends live next door—
sometimes they move interstate.
and group chats become
five individual phone calls.

showing up starts to look
less like dive bars
and more like
doctor's appointments.

we cannot curate our friendships,
but it is the least cinematic times
in which you learn
who truly cares for you.

and at the end of a long day,
all that matters
is knowing
they will be there for you.

**things they don't tell you
about friendships growing up**

a) the most important conversations of your life will happen in a parked car.
b) independence isn't admirable, it's lonely.
c) you can't be a good friend to anyone if you're trying to be a good friend to everyone.
d) if you want someone to trust you, you have to trust them with something first. there's no way around it.
e) some friendships you will simply fall into, some you will need to fight for.
f) when life hits, you will take turns being the better friend. just make sure you don't leave it too long to take your turn.

old messages:

                    i'm just going to grab a few
                          things on my way back

your chocolate almonds are
half price

my targeted ads are more
your snacks than mine

go look at the sky right now!

it looks like it'll be getting
dark soon

when are you coming home?

ghost endings

i am not a fan of endings, but if something has to end, i prefer it go out with a bang. i don't like things that trail off until they vanish into nothingness. i want the big fight, the graduation party, the long kiss goodbye. nothing hurts more than an ending with a question mark, a final chapter left mid-

the texts i didn't send you today:

a)

it's really embarrassing when you sink far into a couch cushion. they act like they're so malleable yet when you stand up they take their time bouncing back.

it's so rude of them.

b)

i am actively trying not to get pregnant but i got my period and was a little disappointed. that's never happened to me before. i don't think i'd make a good mother but i think if i were made a mother, i'd be a good one.

does that make sense?

c)

my nan is in the hospital. she keeps saying she's ready to go home (she doesn't mean to her own bed). i know i should want that for her. it's just that i can't stop thinking about how when she passes, that'll be it.

a whole generation of my family gone.

d)

i've got to call my big sister. i've got to tell my mum i love her. i've got to tell my friend i'm okay that he wants to be part of our family.

i've always thought of him as family anyway.

e)

i boiled the kettle but i only have little teacups left and it's a big-mug kind of day. i could wash up but i could also use a bowl instead. that's french, right?

what do you think i should do?

f)

i'm not the most qualified to talk about rejection. i've gotten every job i've interviewed for and everyone i've loved has loved me back. still, there's the series of texts i haven't sent today because i'm too scared you'll leave me on

read.

g)

i'm a little emotional (see text b)
but you are missing from me.
tu me manques. that's french,
right? i think you're meant to say
that to your lover but you know
what i mean.

h)

you always know what i mean.

i)

wish you were here.

how can i disagree?

nowadays when we meet for coffee, we just can't connect like we used to. it's not from a lack of trying. you turn your phone off and leave it on the table to show me you're here, but neither of us are here like we used to be. i don't know what to say so i comment on how you got a new phone. "yeah," you say, "i had to." then, as if it is no big deal, you add, "everything is built to break nowadays, isn't it?" we lock eyes in that moment. neither of us say anything, but you know what i'm thinking. *looking at us, how can i disagree?*

talk

have you ever had a big friendship grow so small that one day you find yourself asking about the weather?

hot chocolates

a dad of three daughters,
you don't always know what to say.
when we're upset, can't find the words
to reassure us it'll all be okay.

when i was thirteen years old,
there was one night i was crying.
you didn't know how to respond
but i could see that you were trying.

you wanted to know why i was upset,
but sometimes it's just hard being thirteen:
friends will break your heart and
you haven't yet found your self-esteem.

my mother and sister were occupied
with problems of their own,
and i told you that you could help them,
i was okay to be left alone.

but you suggested we go out
and get drinks from a café,
which was big because i've never
seen you in one to this day.

you prefer to be away from people,
and honestly that night i did too.
i got in the car and laughed because
you took us to the mcdonald's drive-thru.

you ordered two hot chocolates
then pulled into an empty spot.
and you didn't say anything
but your gesture said a lot.

we were there for around an hour
while i cried my heart out in the car,
and i dreamed of getting older
with my problems oh so far.

well i am all grown up now,
it's been ten years since that night.
i have an apartment and a big-girl job
and everything is going alright.

so tell me why i'm sitting here
crying about the same old silly things:
friends who have broken my heart
and a runaway self-esteem.

i don't live with you anymore,
don't need you in the way i used to.
you're also ten years older,
soon it'll be me taking care of you.

i love this life but can i be honest?
sometimes it's just hard being twenty-three.
and i'll be fine tomorrow but for tonight,
do you want to get hot chocolates with me?

the all-stop night train

i wish i could dream about made-up monsters. my nightmares materialise as nostalgia. last night i had a dream that i graduated from every season of life i've ever had. i had ceremonies for high school and every job and every friendship and the only other house i've ever called home.

i took a train and travelled from place to place, person to person. and as i made my way across the landscape of my life so far, i spent a few minutes in each location, as though it was normal to be back on bean bags in a living room that no longer exists or belly laughing with classmates you haven't heard from in seven years.

i was surprised by who i missed—each blubber and tear flowing into the next as i painted wild colours on cardboard forts with my childhood best friend and taped up christmas gifts with old co-workers at the card store. but i was even more surprised by who i didn't. people i must have dreamed about so much that their absence doesn't ache anymore. and it's easier to manage the memories.

i have a bad habit of telling people when i have a dream about them. taking pleasure as we pick it apart together like freudian detectives. but there are people i dream about that i know i cannot or should not reach out to. that whatever my role in their life, i've played my final scene. but that won't stop me from uttering a quick prayer for them in the early hours of the morning.

what do you call it when the thing you want the most is the thing you're most afraid of? the best and worst thing you could give me is an album with photos of the butterfly bedspread i had when i was eight and every car dashboard i've stared at while admitting things to the person in the driver's seat. i get scared when i think of something i haven't thought about in years. like that memory was falling off the edges of my subconscious and i've grabbed it by its hairs. it hurts, but what am i made of if not memories?

when my grandfather's mind was fading, the last thing he said to me was "keep going. you'll get there." it made no sense at the time, but they're words i've been holding on to. i can't forget the few things he didn't. what a gift it is to remember.

in my dream, the train was on a tight schedule. so after a few precious minutes at every station, i had to say my ceremonious goodbyes. shed tears for the short time i shared there and hop back on the train. make my slow departure to the next season.

i woke up weeping. i woke up in a place i love with my husband sleeping peacefully next to me. what do you call it when you're living your favourite season of your life so far and you couldn't have gotten here if you stayed living in old ones but you couldn't have gotten here if you skipped them either?

right before i woke up, i started moving into the unknown ahead of me. i heard a familiar voice call out, "keep going. you'll get there." i stuck my head out the train's back window. saw everyone i've ever loved waving me on.

the ride

we don't slow down because
if we did
it might give
the grief in our lungs
a chance to breathe
itself back to life.

it might allow the tidal wave
of missing people to finally
crash down on us.
we might get pummelled by
the memories we tried
to bury beneath the sand.

if only
life happened to us in
bite-sized pieces.
or the ocean delivered
itself to us in bottles.
or we got a second chance
to catch up.

grief grazes
the empty spaces between
our fingers like grains,
but we don't slow down.

because we think it hurts less
to spend our lives
holding our breath

than getting swept up in
the ride.

intimate

i don't see you anymore,
but i still have the bookmark you gave me.
it's been pressed into poem after poem.
a thing of wanderlust,
it has travelled so many worlds,
slept with stories,
made love to language.

anyone who has ever been part of my life
is still part of me in some vastly mysterious
and deeply intimate way.

second-hand store

you do not have to be sentimental to agree that all things have a story. curiosity isn't always born from kindness—occasionally it comes from a place of cruelty. because sometimes you wonder, don't you? how this six-dollar skirt in the second-hand store ever got made in the first place. i'd purchase it just out of pity.

but at some point, it must have seen the light of day. it could have been on dates. could be in photographs on the walls of people still in love. we outgrow our possessions (and i hope evolve in style), but they do not leave our stories behind.

and moving on doesn't have to come from a place of cruelty—sometimes it is kind. i donated all the things you gave me. it was time. but i will not leave our stories behind.

rivers of time

i fell asleep in linen sheets
and woke up in a fright.
did you know that you had visited
in a dream throughout the night?

you came and told me why
i haven't seen you in a while.
and in that blissful midnight hour
we found a way to reconcile.

but when i awoke i discovered
you were still an unsolved crime:
i suspect that you were simply
stolen by the rivers of time.

i know the reason you revealed
in my subconscious state
was not the actual reason
i haven't seen you as of late.

but my mind, it draws conclusions—
we're a problem it wants to solve.
so it wrote a simple story
to count your absence as resolved.

you'd laugh if you ever heard it
(though i don't think you'll get the chance).
we seem to only ever speak
under just one circumstance:

a text on your birthday,
and another one on mine,
as though every night we spent talking
is now lost in the mists of time.

and dear friend, i am frightened
for i see what my mind is trying to do:
turning you from someone i know
into someone i once knew.

because what if i'm not ready
to write the end of you and me?
what if, on my birthday,
you're the text i'm waiting to see?

i know that makes me foolish—
friendship is a fickle thing.
we're moving on with our lives
and people get lost in the upswing.

        (but if you ever find you're not ready,
        if i ever visit you in a dream,
        just say the word, i'll swim through time,
        i'll battle its rivers upstream.

        on its banks, i'm sure we'll find
        a way to reconcile.
        and it will not matter that
        i haven't seen you in a while.)

i'm sorry

you unlocked a longing deep within me.
i know that does not mean you're the key.

surprise me with a friendship.

one that's wild and green.
that together grows us into
who we could not have been.

surprise me with a friendship.
planted in this place.
that will lead to a flourishing
which colours every space.

surprise me with a friendship.
that cannot be framed.
which sprawls bravely out the edges
when it tries to be tamed.

God bless this budding friendship.
that one day will bloom.
i will try to be patient,
but i hope to meet them soon.

rearranging

people don't surprise me like they used to.
but it can't be because human nature
has changed.

must be that when someone hands me
parts of themself, i decide
how they must be arranged.

give me a piece,
i'll build you a picture—
that's just my imagination.

but perhaps i need to let people
play out naturally
instead of creating my own narration.

what if i told someone a story
(just the start of what i'm about),
and from that tiny puzzle piece
they thought they had me
figured out?

because i know in my heart of hearts
that people are great mysteries.
that even they cannot read
all the layers of their stories.

so lately i've been asking
a string of wildly irrelevant questions.
and people are surprising me
with even wilder reflections.

i am apologising left   right   and
                          centre
for the people i thought i knew.

throwing out all my assumptions.
starting the picture
                      anew.

library card

i saw you again
outside the public library.

i was sitting
on the ridiculously proportioned steps—
the council's poor attempt
to make concrete spaces
appear like architecture.

you were sitting,
back straight against the glass doors.
unfazed by the sharpness in may's air.
maybe, like me,
you forgot for the third time this month
that the library doesn't open until nine-thirty.

i was trying to get comfortable,
shifting and sighing
at the inconvenience to my Very Busy Day.
my hand was rummaging through my bag
for my library card,
another forgotten thing.

you possessed an unfamiliar patience.
you did not stir
at the chaos of commuters storming past.
or the teenagers darting to school.

you were reading a novel i couldn't
make out the title of.
but the cover was orange.
breakfast at tiffany's maybe.
the adventures of huckleberry finn.

i wanted to know,
'what is this world you are caught up in?
and can i go there with you too?'

i wanted to say,
'excuse me, but i forgot my library card,
can i borrow some stories off you?'

because you are reading as though the pages
are the passageway to peace.
and i want nothing more than
to step inside your mind. find
how it is that you got there.

could you spare the morning to share
all the secret, insignificant details of your life?

tell me everything that has happened
to bring you to the library
on this freezing autumn day.

but the glass doors opened
and you walked in
before i'd even worked out what to say.

never mind,
i found what i was looking for.

i smiled,
and went the other way.

silver braids

what stories must be tied up
in your silver braids.
all i want to do
is spend the afternoon pulling
poetry out of your hair.

our shared fabric

connection doesn't always come the way you want it to. it's not always the blanket over your shoulders on a cold night. or the rug pulled out under your secrets. not all people are meant to be the calls you make when you have news or the partner to the plans you've devised. but that doesn't make them less significant. i'd like to pick a fight with whoever made the word 'friend' and left it to cover all the different compositions of relationship. relationships fade and form and weave new colours into our shared fabric. until you can't label the fibres from which you are made. but you know it's a blend of the people you've connected with on the way.

furious curiosity

every now and then you meet someone
who is not quite a friend
but could be.

time is painful with them.
but only because you know
you will soon need to part.

you never want to run out of their stories.
never want to close the book.
you want to learn them inside out.

but it is not your right.

oh, it is the people we are most drawn to
whom we withdraw from.

for we want too much.
and they will never be enough
for our furious curiosity.

do you have the time?

i can learn a lot about a person
from the way they talk about time.

if time is something linear or cyclical.
if they talk about their life as though
it goes through seasons the way nature does
or if it is something ever growing,
always moving forward.

if they talk about failure as though
it is several steps back on their timeline
or simply a change of course.

if they describe the day according to
the clock or to the sky.
was it five am or dawn?
eight pm or twilight?

i love to notice whether they speak as though
the hours ahead are an opportunity
or if they are an order.

i love to wonder,
is time something that carries them
or something they are carrying?

i don't really know what to do with this knowledge.
i just like having it.

i just like the thought that i can tell
something. other than the time.

what the rain can teach us about kindness

the rain doesn't know there is a drought. how can it?
it is only rain.

the rain doesn't know it is something we are
desperate for. that it has been the subject of
thousands of prayers. how can it? it is only rain.

it doesn't know that today, people will seek refuge in
thousands of small spaces. that we will make
comments on how hard it is pouring, and
conversations will take shape in the same way the rain
does: a drop on an awning that will wash down the
roadside that will reach the rivers. the rain doesn't
know about kindness. it doesn't know that it is
another thing we are desperate for. the rain will never
know how many lives it touched today. how can it?
it is only rain.

stranger on the early morning train II

i met you four years ago
in the pouring rain,
had a good conversation
on the early morning train.

we covered so much ground
across the city's bumpy track.
sure threw my heart for a spin,
took a while for it to come back.

you reminded me of someone
i was trying hard to let go,
and the grief just came pouring,
an ache i wished i did not know.

i felt finally ready
for a goodbye i didn't know how to say,
so i wrote it in a poem
called 'stranger on the early morning train'.

i published it in a book,
got messages from more strangers,
who knew of the same loss
and were carrying the remainders.

they shared a little of their lives,
just like you shared a little of yours.
the poem gave them courage
to gently shut old doors.

i thought you'd never know this
until in a town where i was new,
i saw someone in the early morning
who reminded me too much of you.

i was surprised you remembered me,
even if you forgot my name.
i considered telling you about the poem,
but it's embarrassing to explain.

so i shook your hand once more,
said i should be on my way.
but you have messed me up again,
i've been thinking about you for days.

some people we journey with,
others we leave behind.
but the time you spend with someone
doesn't equal time they're on your mind.

meeting you stayed with me
long after the train left the station,
and it's mortifying to be
on the other side of that equation.

to you, i am a moment,
to me, you are a milestone.
you erased me from your memory,
i engraved you into my own.

and oh, i tried to make it balance,
but i love the fall-out from the fail,
so if it's okay with you,
i'm letting this one tip the scales.

how to catch light

1) firstly, wait until the very end of the day. until you are sure the darkness would swallow even your shadow.

2) put some comfortable shoes on.

3) take a friend, or don't. it isn't likely to matter as you won't be alone for long.

4) find a hill near your city and climb it. don't look back until you are certain you have reached the top.

5) when you are sure that you are ready, utter a tiny prayer for your heart to open. please, do not skip this step.

6) now turn around in awe. notice how it looks like someone has tipped over a jar and spilt out the night sky. how there are tiny stars pooled all over the city.

7) cast your open heart out in a wide net and see what it returns. catch light from pedestrian crossings. streetlights. the television show in a stranger's window.

8) shrink at how insignificant we all seem from afar. marvel at how bright we are together.

9) store all this light in a safe place. keep it for when you need to remember this tiny galaxy. and how miraculous it is that we are all swimming in the same universe.

window

the light teaches me just how much can spill through a small window of opportunity.

forgive me

forgive me for the times
i missed my cue.
when the opportunities were plenty
but my responses few.

forgive me for the details
i didn't piece together.
for the suffering i would have seen
if my attention was better.

forgive me for not looking
because i didn't want to find.
never let me blink away
another chance to be kind.

silence

there is a lady on my walk to the station who is always tending to her plants. her apartment backs onto a park and i wonder if she ever aches at the sound of laughter coming through her garden.

i wonder if she has someone to laugh with.
i wonder if she lost someone she used to tend to.

we always smile at each other.

(i hope one day one of us thinks of something to say.)

weird

when i was in high school, i used to always tell my friend to buy me coffee. he would always tell me to polish his shoes. of course, we did neither. i don't even remember why we said them. we say weird things when we are teenagers.

once, i was having a hard time. i told no one. he noticed. walked straight up to me in the quad. said nothing. later, he would come up to me with a hot coffee from the canteen. press a fistful of sugar packets into my hand. i tried to say something but he had already walked away.

a few months later, he would take his turn at a hard time. we had already graduated high school. i did not see him often. i went to the supermarket just to buy some shoe polish. sent it in the mail. we do weird things when we are teenagers.

we didn't speak much after that. i didn't know how to love. i don't think he forgave me.

most of the time, i don't know the right words to say or the best thing to do when people are hurting. admittedly, it's been a long time since i've tried.

but a few weeks ago, a friend told me something her therapist said: at the start of each day, we each have a dozen oranges. we use them as energy for different tasks, and if we are lucky, we go to bed with a few left in our hands. but if you are grieving, you use most of your oranges just getting out of bed in the morning. my friend said she felt all out of oranges. squeezed dry. we say weird things when we are adults.

i nodded. said nothing. i went to the supermarket just to buy a dozen oranges. brought them to her house. we do weird things when are adults.

i didn't know how to love. she forgave me.

since then, i've started to keep a note in my phone of the coffees people order. just in case, one day, i need to press one into their palms.

the awkward silence

it's never bothered me much. am i afraid you may think i am not the pinnacle of eloquence? not an agile thinker capable of putting both of us at ease? i can tell you right now i'm neither.

i mean, there are times i wish i could speak like i write: a pen that never leaves the page. but if i didn't have a little awkwardness to my name, i never would have discovered how to make magic out of silence. it's my greatest trick.

sure, sometimes people will scramble. and you've got the classics. the *how was the drive*, the *what's on for tomorrow*, and let's not forget the *hot today, isn't it?* there is poetry in the pivot too. but,

and yes, i am leaving an uncomfortable amount of silence here for effect. if you wait a moment, you may find people have more to say.

you may find that people will want to share more of their heart. because it is the most incredible ideas that seem impossible. the most-loved tales that seem too long to tell.

and this is not a party trick. you won't impress anybody. you'll have to learn how to hold confessions that make you uncomfortable. opinions that you vehemently oppose. stories that will create the kind of silence you wish was awkward. the silence of i-am-so-sorry-i-don't-know-what-i-could-possibly-say.

but you will love people. oh, you will love them in an awkward, silent, all-consuming, beautiful way.

mischievous

the sky is writing up a storm.
that mischievous storyteller
wants to see what parts of humanity
he can dredge up
by adding a little rain.

sometimes,
i like to make people feel comfortable
with small talk and social pleasantries.

other times,
i take my lead from the sky.

i want to know about the décor in your living room. the books you own but have never read. i want to know why the bookmark is on page eleven. why you stopped reading. if there was a lousy sentence or you fell asleep or there was a knock on the door. i want to know your heartbreak. the reason why you have certain quotes stuck to your fridge. which names come to mind when i say the word love. what about hurt? are they the same? i want to know about the memories tucked behind your ear. if there are other places you call home. because i know we are already inside this place you call yours. but in so many ways, i am still waiting.

i want you to let me in.

eight billion saltwater vessels

if you told me to follow my heart, i would tell you that i have spent years running in the other direction. and that everyone, in their own way, does the same. i would tell you that, despite my best efforts to keep it still, it is the one that follows me.

how do you guard a heart that is more saltwater than flesh? i try to stop it from overflowing, but some days it feels as though i am bursting with a secret that no longer wants to be kept.

if you showed me a picture of the universe, it would not be enough to convince me of anything. because i can show you how, in every person, there is a universe. and we are not so small after all.

if you listen carefully, you can hear the evidence. we are only ever expanding. it starts as the sound of running water. streams lead to waterfalls lead to lakes lead to rivers lead to the realisation that my heart has always been an ocean:

that we are eight billion saltwater vessels

and yet, too afraid to leave the shore.

fable

please listen carefully to the following fable: one morning i was in a café with my umbrella by my table. a man came up to poke fun, because hadn't i seen the clear sky? but by afternoon it was pouring, and my umbrella kept me dry. the storm came out of nowhere, as storms are wont to do. and people howled with laughter as they had no choice but to run through. i saw the throngs of humans getting drenched on their way home. i've never felt smarter, safer, or more utterly alone.

answer me this riddle: if you prepare for the worst, does that make the worst any better, or does it just make the better worse?

what the light will do

there's an elephant in your
coffee cup.
an obstruction of view.
friend, it's been some time now
since i've gotten to
see you.

you've got your shame.
God knows i've got
mine too.

but shame only thrives
in the darkness of secrecy:
let's see what the light
will do.

intoxicating

trust is a kind of intoxication.

i love to watch
words fall recklessly out
of mouths at midnight,
everything once bottled up
turned to broken shards
for another to hold.

i hate to watch
people wake up
the next morning,
full of regret,
feeling sick at the thought
of how much they shared.

is it so awful?
this being known?

are you going to walk your heart
safely to its shallow grave

or let it run wild on the grounds
of spilled inhibitions?

safe to try

it may take me a long time
to articulate my heart.

i may stutter. or use
a thousand useless words.

but if you don't understand
anything i am saying,

at least know that,
around you,

i feel safe enough to try.

synonyms

you think that because i am a writer
i am a walking thesaurus.

you ask me,

"what's another word for bittersweet?"
"what's another word for adoration?"
"what's another word for safety?"

but my vocabulary is not built
from big, dusty books:
it is founded in friendship.

we have spent so much time together
that your sayings are mine.

another word for bittersweet is
"see you later, alligator."

another word for adoration is
"you're the goosiest of geese."

another word for safety is
"goodnight, vegemite."

there are so many synonyms in our structure
that they are near inseparable now.

i am a walking thesaurus.

another word for me is you.

things i didn't need to know:

you found a place you can get refills for your favourite pen. you slid into the bath with a chai tea and got the temperature wrong for both. your co-worker made a bad pun while you were at your company lawn bowls. you found a feather that made you wish you owned a quill pen. you just hung out your washing. you used to love madonna. then you didn't. now you do again. you had a dream you were being chased by a giant koala that only wanted to hug you.

i did not need to know any of that.

i am so, so glad you told me.

day trip

someone interprets 'we're leaving just after 7' as be ready on the hour; someone interprets it as the time to finally get in the shower.

someone packs five homemade sandwiches in bags you can reuse; *someone forgets to wear shoes…*

someone spends the whole trip on maps, finding the fastest route to the location; someone starts the number plate game, couldn't care less about the destination.

someone sneaks in to pay for petrol after perpetually complaining that they're poor; someone sends their bank account details for the bag of chips they bought at the station store.

but on the way back, you're all so happy tired, tuckered out, and sun-kissed, that no one cares anymore about the piggyback over bindis or all the highway exits that were missed.

half the car is napping, the aux cord stays plugged into the same person's phone. and it's a weird mash-up of five different genres that you listen to on the way home.

you think that one of these days they'll change their mind about your quirks, decide they've had enough of you. but somehow, it hasn't happened yet. *somehow, they never do.*

brothers

i love my girl friendships.
but have you gone for long
car rides with guys and heard
them soften as they share about
why they love certain songs? have
you ever been asked if you're
okay so sincerely that it
makes you tear up
even if you are?
have you ever been
mocked so mercilessly
that you can't even be
offended because you are
touched by how you are so
deeply known? have you ever
befriended someone when they
were a boy and, over the years,
witnessed him become a man?

i was not born with brothers.
now, i have many.

sisters

i adore my male friendships.
but have you ever gone for a
car ride with a girl just to scream
songs you couldn't get concert tickets
for? have you asked how last night
went and received two dozen
voice notes to debrief?
have you ever been
followed into
the bathroom
because your girls
noticed you weren't
okay and gave you a hug
you didn't even know you
needed? have you ever looked
at someone who is becoming the
most beautiful woman and felt
nearly breathless with pride?

some sisters i was born with.
others, i have found.

envy

when my heart was coloured green, i looked out for the weeds in others' gardens. without realising, this habit became the invasive weed in mine.

the garden that she's growing

in my neighbourhood,
there are roses bursting
with colour,
but i am losing the desire
to pick them.

i don't need to own things
to appreciate them.

her charisma.
his talent.
her thoughtfulness.
his strength.

to each his own garden.

lately, i've been spending
less time in mine.
no longer out of jealousy,
just to linger
among the roses' perfume.

how beautiful the street that blooms.

disjointed

community is a craft.
the art of patching something
together out of pieces.
the bringing of disjointed things
as they are and,
with care and creativity,
making something beautiful.

passenger

it's a tuesday night. i'm sitting in the passenger seat as my husband drives us home from a house where we have found some random people from a local church and decided to hitch our lives to theirs. so we meet every tuesday to hear about their joys and sorrows and pray for each other's lives which we may not have much in common with (at least, not at first glance). but Love has taken us here. just as it has gifted us our marriage, it has also led us to a new town which feels more like ours with every passing day.

it's a tuesday night. this is what life is: sitting in the passenger seat of Love's car as it drives us slowly home. sometimes this lends itself to fear and grabbing the wheel. but other times (the best of times), Love will drive us past houses where new friendships will be made. it will take us the scenic route where we will discover a tree-lined street of shops shut many hours before. there are fairy lights wrapped around each tree, and we will come to call it our 'tuesday treat' and savour the sweetness of its honey glow.

it's a tuesday night. our favourite Passenger song is playing on the car radio. we are so close to our beloved apartment, but i am already falling softly asleep. i feel safe here. i will let Love steer.

third places

when people ask where i live,
i know they're really asking
what i write as my mailing address.

but to me where i live
is all these other places,
for which i consider myself blessed:

a coffee shop (or five) where
i can start my day right.

a bridge where
i can walk with friends in the last of the daylight.

a pilates studio where
i can laugh off the pain.

a pool where
i hurriedly sidestep swimmers in my lane.

a church where
i can worship alongside other voices.

a library where
i can work in the company of soft noises.

a park where
i admire the old, ever-changing trees.

a beach where
i breathe deep just to taste the salty breeze.

how are you, really? II

i hope when someone asks me about my life and how it is going, i talk about the health of my brothers, the jobs of my sisters, the joys of my parents. i want to talk about the struggles of my friends, the mission of my church, the celebrations of my neighbours overseas.

oh, my life is so much bigger than me.

welcome mat

three summers ago, i started renting my first place. it was a tiny unit down the road from the cemetery, but i loved it so much that when i couldn't stay there, i began to miss it. i ached for the musty smell of the carpet and obnoxious pattern of the curtains. i put so much thought and time into making this place somewhere i could belong.

then one day, i had an idea. i decided that if i was going to build a home, if i was going to buy a cheese knife, laundry detergent, and a pot plant to sit under the leaking pipe, i would also continue to build other homes that were perhaps less conspicuous.

i would make a home out of my best friend and make sure i kept visiting, at least often enough no cobwebs grew over my memory of her co-worker's names. i would make a home out of the beach, collect my mail from the sand, and always find hundreds of new love letters from God with my name on the address.

and most importantly, i would try to make a home for other people. lay out a welcome mat wherever i happened to be—with a warm greeting to a shopper in the city bookstore or a repositioned bag on the bus as an offer to another exhausted commuter.

i decided i would do everything in my power to build so many different homes, so that no matter where i was or who i happened to be with, we would feel as though we had come to an extra plate set at the dinner table. as if there were someone near us saying, 'welcome. there is so much room for you here.'

peppermint

i don't think there are many things more beautiful than keeping a flavour of tea you don't like in your kitchen cupboard, purely because someone you love does.

what i wish i could say to my 21-year-old self:

you do not need a career.
you need money, yes,
but there is money to be found
in a whole myriad of workplaces.
don't be afraid to try them.

you do not need a friend group.
you need friends, yes,
but there are people waiting
in the most unlikely of places.
don't be afraid to love them.

whatever you do,
don't believe the lie
that you are a piece of the puzzle
just waiting to be slot into
a place where you belong.
you will not find it.
but, if you stop trying
to squeeze yourself into
gaps that are not your shape,
you may just realise that
you are capable of
changing the picture,
and belonging doesn't matter
so much anymore.

you could go anywhere,
you know?
you could do anything.
you'll be ok.
you've got nothing but time.

longing

the day after my birthday, i watched a man in the bookstore answer a group facetime call. half a dozen friends sung happy birthday out of time, out of tune, out of love. this moment became a lump in my throat. a lump that grew and grew until it became the size of me. i soon came to know it by a new name: Longing.

Longing and i became well-acquainted over time. i walked with it for a while. it wasn't trying to embarrass me but i was embarrassed to be around it. because i felt shame for not being satisfied with the relationships i had. and probably more shame for not already having the relationships i wanted.

but Longing did not go away at mere will. nor did it leave when i packed its bags. worked hard to make it known i wanted it gone. i decided that if Longing was going to stick around, i might as well listen to it.

Longing had a lot to teach me. it showed me so much about myself that it felt like we had known each other much longer. in time, i came to know Longing as a friend.

i barely noticed Longing leave. but one time, i was in a room with people whom i had started to love with my whole heart. people who i will call on their birthdays, who will call me on mine. i was laughing and laughing and out of the corner of my eye, i caught Longing standing in the doorway. it looked back at me, smiling. i nodded, tears in my eyes.

then Longing slipped out the door.

surrounded by flowers

i spent a long time looking for community. i thought all about the kinds of people i wanted around me and what life would look like when lived in tune with the rhythms of others.

in the end, i had to stop obsessively worrying about it. i simply planted some seeds. some coffee dates. some texts. some suggestions of walks and wines and other wonderful ways to waste time.

learning to be okay with waste was the hardest thing. to come home sometimes with the overwhelming feeling that i never wanted to do it again. (i learned to be okay with the humiliation of being on the other side of that too.) of course, i also learned more about the ambiguity of adulthood and finding people you feel aligned with in spirit yet never in schedule.

but then there were people i learned to love deeply whom i never thought i would. i felt loved by people in a way that i wasn't deserving of. our lives overflowed into each other's rhythms. people became my tuesday nights and saturday mornings and thursday evenings. but also sprawled outside of schedules and became spontaneous trips to the ocean, five-am sleepy voice messages, and conversations so good i sacrificed half my sleep.

i stopped pursuing people i thought i could love and closing my heart off to people i thought i had nothing in common with.

i allowed people to surprise me.

i stopped trying to label people as best friends and close friends and good friends and friends and acquaintances. i just lived life with a heart open to the mysteries of relationship.

i gave it time.

one day i woke up and realised
i was surrounded by flowers.

community is just grace
overgrown.

an abundance of oranges

a few years ago, God gave me a dream i did not understand. it was of an orange tree. so ripe and ready that fruit was falling overhead. i did not know how to interpret it. but each time i passed an orange tree, i'd check for fallen fruit below.

i could have collected crates by now. i'd ponder how the bones of these trees were not designed to carry the weight. how the harvest was so heavy they had to hand it down.

i gave away oranges. got them in return. i tried to count them. but my life became so overrun by oranges that eventually i had to admit it was not a math problem but a miracle. that goodness grows even when i don't have a hand in it. and grace has been here.

i confess,
i still don't entirely understand
what God is doing.

but i often have big dreams.
ones so big it'll take time
for me to grow into them.

these days,
i fall asleep dreaming
of nothing but
oranges.

a letter to the girl about to turn twenty-five

i hope all your days get derailed. and you will plead with God for productivity, and he will remind you with his patient voice that he has put a new vision in you. i hope you shed your own story layer by layer and surrender your pride to his service.

i hope all your daydreams get dissected. and you find more and more of the stuff you are trying to hide from God. and he will remind you with his patient voice that he has put a new vision in you. i hope you peel open your desires layer by layer and surrender your pride to his service.

i hope that as you grow older, you grow younger in spirit. become more like a child with each passing day. i hope you look up to your Father from a place low to the ground. listen to his ever-patient voice. know his everlasting love. and surrender your little heart to the arms that are lifting you.

Acknowledgements

I *really* didn't want to write this section. And nearly didn't. I've always held a somewhat romantic view of people and the way we paint each other's memories. But the process of writing this book took it to a whole new level. I have never been so aware of the tiny, monumental ways people have shaped my life.

Here's my dilemma: it would be impossible to write down the names of every person who inspired part of this book. Yet, writing acknowledgements only feels overwhelming because I've been overwhelmingly blessed. So I need to say something.

Thank you to Aidan, Alicia, Andrew, Aqeel, Emma, Faye, Georgia, Hannah, Isabelle, Josie, Joyce, and Sarah for sharing your thoughts on the draft of this book. Thank you for encouraging, challenging, and (though you may not know it) inspiring me.

Eleana, thank you for all your help editing this book. I love how the Lord has woven our stories together in his timing. You are, and will continue to be, a blessing to the poetry community.

Matthew, every day you go out of your way to support me in my passions and ensure I am taken care of. You created the perfect cover for this book, but honestly, I had no doubt that you would. I know you'll always come through for me in more ways than one and I'm so grateful for that.

I have to acknowledge God for the beautiful stories
he has been writing—some of which, by his grace,
I have shared in this book, and some of which,
I believe in my bones, are to come.

There are a few less specific but by no means less
important notes of gratitude I want to share.

To those who have taught me more about what
friendship and family mean: you're everything to me.

To those who have believed in me as a writer: your
encouragement is felt.

To those who have read this book: I am so grateful
you're here. I hope these words have meant
something to you.

About the Author

Rachel H is a poet and writer based in Sydney, Australia.

She is usually found with a coffee in one hand and a pen in the other. She's obsessed with stories and loves equipping other writers to share their own.

Her previous works include *Fleeting Things*, 2020, and *Making Whole*, 2022.

rachelhuckel.com | @rachelhuckel

www.ingramcontent.com/pod-product-compliance
Lightning Source LLC
Chambersburg PA
CBHW022013290426
44109CB00015B/1160